We are the Dyspraxia Champions!

This book was inspired by ADHD Is Our Superpower by Soli Lazarus!

If you have ADHD, you might struggle with concentrating in school, or sitting still, or remembering instructions. But ADHD is also a superpower.

You will meet different girls and boys with ADHD who can do amazing things. They also let you know how grown-ups can help. You might have some of these strengths too!

Soli Lazarus runs the Yellow Sun consultancy providing support to families with a child with ADHD. She also delivers ADHD training to primary schools and was previously a teacher and SENCO with 30 years' experience.

Also in the series

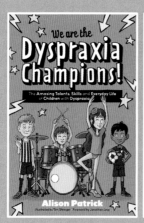

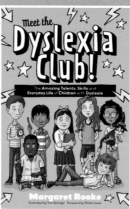

We are the Dyspraxia Champions!

The Amazing Talents, Skills and Everyday Life of Children with Dyspraxia

Alison Patrick

Illustrated by Tim Stringer • Foreword by Jonathan Levy

Jessica Kingsley Publishers
London and Philadelphia

Firstly, to my family, with love.
Secondly, to dyspraxia, autism & ADHD
– without you, I wouldn't be me.

First published in Great Britain in 2025 by Jessica Kingsley Publishers
An imprint of John Murray Press

1

The fonts, layout and overall design of this book have been prepared
according to dyslexia-friendly principles. At JKP we aim to make
our books' content accessible to as many readers as possible.

A CIP catalogue record for this title is available from the
British Library and the Library of Congress

ISBN 978 1 83997 910 1
eISBN 978 1 83997 911 8

Printed and bound in China by Leo Paper Products Ltd

Jessica Kingsley Publishers
Carmelite House
50 Victoria Embankment
London EC4Y 0DZ

www.jkp.com

John Murray Press
Part of Hodder & Stoughton Ltd
An Hachette Company

Foreword

By Jonathan Levy, former Dyspraxia Foundation Chair

As former chair of Dyspraxia Foundation, the UK's only charity dedicated to supporting people with dyspraxia, and as a person with dyspraxia myself, it is an honour to have been asked to contribute in a small way to this great book.

Personally speaking, I didn't particularly enjoy or do very well in school. I recall being told that due to having dyspraxia, I might never be able to do X, Y and Z, and this hurt. I was good at coming last and felt that I stood out from others, so I sometimes wished that I was more 'normal'. I often felt talked down to, and, as I look back, I realize that the seemingly low expectations affected me significantly.

They made me resolute in aiming to play my part in breaking down barriers, proving people wrong and achieving my goals, and since then, I've done exactly that, being at the front of various initiatives in the charity sector, and politics, founding businesses, serving in leadership roles, being elected to local government, public speaking, appearing on TV, winning awards and all sorts of other things. I know I've achieved a good amount, but I'm just one of many happy and successful dyspraxic people.

Lived experience is a powerful thing, and as both an education professional and an expert through lived experience, Alison is well qualified to write this book. I was immediately drawn to the title, **We are the Dyspraxia Champions!** because although life with dyspraxia can certainly be challenging, there is a good amount to champion. Yes, people with dyspraxia often struggle with balance, organization, and spatial awareness amongst other things, but they possess many great qualities too, and the four children in this book, Eva, Raj, Leo and Ellis, are shining examples of this, and each conveys ambition and hopes for their future.

This book isn't just helpful for children with dyspraxia. If you're a parent or professional, then this book will benefit you too as it provides helpful guidance on how you can support children with dyspraxia at home or in the classroom. It doesn't gloss over things, but gives good practical tips. I related to a lot covered in this book, and I expect you will too.

Dyspraxia affects around 5 per cent of school-age children, so in every class of 30, there's likely to be at least one child affected by dyspraxia, often undiagnosed, which means it's more common than many people realize.

No matter how you're feeling about dyspraxia right now, please know that it absolutely doesn't have to be a barrier to opportunity and fulfilment. There are many successful people with dyspraxia, including household names whom you can find by searching online. Each person with dyspraxia has succeeded in their own way, often having to overcome various obstacles and work harder than their peers, but success often means more when you've really had to work for it.

Whatever your link to dyspraxia, celebrate every accomplishment and have faith that life will turn out well.

Jonathan Levy

Former Dyspraxia Foundation Chair

Why I Wrote This Book

Hi, I'm Alison. Before you start reading about the children in this book, here's a bit about me.

I know a lot about dyspraxia because I've had dyspraxia since the day I was born. I also have autism and ADHD. Some of the traits that go with dyspraxia, autism and ADHD can make life tricky to navigate, but some are my superpowers – focusing on stuff in detail and thinking outside the box. I wouldn't be without these superpowers for one minute.

I wrote this book so that you can find out more about dyspraxia, and the ADHD, autism or dyslexia that can be a part of you too. I want you to be aware of the strengths that come with dyspraxia, and to have strategies for handling the weaknesses that can coexist with them.

You will read about four children, and they'll tell you about their life at school and home. You can read about them in any order:

- Eva is dyspraxic.
- Raj is dyspraxic and dyslexic.
- Leo has dyspraxia and ADHD.
- Ellis is dyspraxic and autistic.

I hope you enjoy this book, and that it helps you to find out more about your dyspraxia and the superpowers that go with it.

Love,

Alison x

Other books by Alison

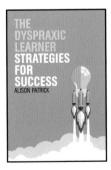

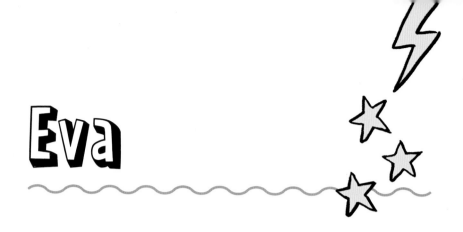

Eva

Hi, my name is Eva — I'm Eva Everton. I live in Edinburgh. I have long, dark curly hair and brown eyes. I am an only child but I have a beautiful black Labrador dog called Howard who is eight years old, and my friends in the street where I live are my brothers and sisters.

I am dyspraxic, but this is not an illness. I think Howard might be dyspraxic too. He can't balance, and when he sits up tall on the kitchen floor, his paws slide. Howard can't catch either, but he is getting better with practice. Howard is a very clever dog. He always uses his sense of smell to track down food, even when no one else can see any food for miles.

Some more fun facts about me. I am the tallest girl in my class at school. I'm seven years old and I'm in year three. My birthday is in February, and so is Howard's. My favourite colour is green, and my favourite food is chicken Kiev. My favourite thing of all is dancing. Mum says I'm good at dancing because my dyspraxia makes me so flexible.

At times dyspraxia can be tricky, but at other times it is my superpower.

My dyspraxia

Let me try to explain a bit more about dyspraxia.

When I was born, I could not swallow and I had to stay in hospital for a few weeks. When I came home, I did not sleep well, so I screamed a lot, and that meant my family did not sleep well either, not even the dog. Howard howled a lot too when I was a baby. Mum says, 'All babies cry a lot. All day and all night, some of them.'

I never crawled. I shuffled along on my bottom instead. My mum was worried because I didn't walk until I was two years old. I went to the hospital to be checked out, but I was OK. It's a dyspraxia thing, bottom shuffling and walking late. Mum says that as soon as I could walk I made up for lost time!

When I went to preschool, I could not hold a pencil or crayons properly. I dropped things and bumped into things a lot. I still bump into things a lot.

At school, my class teacher thought I should see an occupational therapist. That's a very long name to remember, so it's called an OT for short. An OT looks at how we do things and ways to make these things easier. I liked the OT – she was fun and I got to throw bean bags across the room!

The OT said that I had dyspraxia. It has been really helpful to know that is why I do some things differently. I get more help at school too.

Dyspraxia affects my balance. I'm very wobbly when I try to balance, but karate at after-school club helps my posture and balance. I love music and dancing too. When I'm dancing, I know dyspraxia is just one part of my life. It doesn't matter if I have 'butterfingers' when I'm catching or throwing, because I am a Dancing Queen. My gran says, 'No one is good at everything, Eva.'

Dyspraxia affects things called fine motor skills and gross motor skills. Let's start with my fine motor skills.

Fine motor skills are about how I hold things.

Unfortunately, fine doesn't mean that they don't cause me any trouble! My mum says I'm clumsy because I break toys, and when I help with the dishes, I break the china and glasses.

It can be fiddly to fasten the buttons on my school shirt. I've got better at that with practice, and I just have to remember not to panic. What's the hurry after all?

That reminds me, I'm a messy eater too, and my school uniform has to be washed a lot. I found the school canteen scary at first, but now my friends are there with me, so it is easier.

I don't mind being clumsy so much now that I know it is because of the dyspraxia.

Gross motor skills are about how I move.

I'm a member of the tree club in the street where I live, beside a park called the Inch. It took me ages to be able to climb the tree just outside my house where I meet my friends Matt, Will and Harriet-Ann. I was scared of the spaces between the branches and how to move between them, and I thought I would fall and break my bones.

But one day I climbed onto the lowest branch, and I just kept climbing. Now I am really good at climbing trees.

I still haven't learned to ride a bike because it's hard to pedal and balance all at once, but my dad said that if I can climb a tree, I can ride a bicycle as well as anyone. So I've started going out with my dad holding on to the back of the bicycle to keep me steady.

One other thing to know about dyspraxia is that I don't judge spaces very well, so I bump into things and stub my toes quite a lot. I always have bruises. At the moment, I have a massive bruise on my elbow from walking into a door frame, a smaller bruise on my leg and a sore toe. Yesterday, I cut my finger opening a can of cola too. And my knees are always grazed because I seem to fall over more than my friends. The school nurse said that I'm a warrior and I should have a medal for bravery on the playground.

Sleeping and eating

There's some stuff that I don't like that my mum calls 'sensory' because it is linked to my senses. I don't like lumpy food like mashed potatoes or stewed fruit. In fact, potatoes must be the worst thing ever invented. I detest boiled potatoes, and it feels like we eat those a lot, almost every day of the week. My mum says that the face I pull when I look at my plate of food makes her sad.

I can be funny about clothes too. The texture has to be right, not bobbly or prickly. I've got a unicorn dressing gown that I have had since I was five, which I wear around the house all the time when I am chilling out. It's cuddly like a teddy bear.

I have got a big bear called Barney to help me sleep at night because I lie awake, and when I do fall asleep, even a tiny noise will wake me up. I don't really like the dark, so I have a baby light in my room. I'm going to stop having a night light when I am eight. Grown-ups don't have lights on at night and I want to be ready for that.

School

You may be wondering if my dyspraxia shows when I am in the classroom. One thing that happens is that I can hear, but I don't always understand what I've heard. If the teacher speaks slowly and repeats what she has said, that helps.

I struggle to focus, but the teacher taps my desk and says 'Eva' and I'm back! I have a hair scrunchie on my wrist that I ping when I know I'm starting to daydream. I don't always know that I have lost focus – that's the problem – and my mind feels fuzzy when I come back.

My handwriting is untidy, and my fingers cramp because holding a pen is awkward. Our headmistress, Mrs Aird, got me a special pen for left-handers when she was on an away day, and that has helped. I also

use a sloped board to rest my paper on and sit in front of the whiteboard so I don't have to crick my neck. I'm learning to touch type so I can be ready for when I have to write more at big school.

I haven't fully cracked reading yet, but I can read a lot of words. I'm in a group for extra help, and my teacher, Mrs Lamberton, says she wants to have me reading every word by the summer.

In year two, the speech therapist helped me because I couldn't say 'th' words. I said 'fink' instead of 'think' and I couldn't spell words like 'though'.

I'm always really tired after school, so when I get home, I watch TV. After tea, I like making collages to relax. I've got collages all over my bedroom wall.

I haven't talked about numbers yet. I'm good at adding, but I can't remember my times tables. I'm at the bottom table for maths, with my friend Nessa. Mum says times tables won't matter so much when I'm older and can focus on the subjects I enjoy, like geography or history.

Oddly, I can't remember my times tables, but I can tell you exactly what I had for tea on the day we went back to school after half-term last year. (It was fish fingers, chips and peas, and then strawberry mousse.) I have an amazing memory for the past, but I would swap it to be better at maths and spelling. I really would.

Friends

I'm shy with people I don't know well, and I'm quiet at school. This can happen with dyspraxia because it can be hard to find the words to join in and play games. It's easy to get left behind if you don't run fast.

Nobody talked to me when I first went to junior school. I don't really like change. But then our TA, Miss Struthers, set up a circle group at playtime and I made friends.

My friends at school are Simone, Nessa and Elena. I'm not always good at knowing when to speak, so I interrupt. Sometimes I mishear and take offence, and then we quarrel, but we always make up, even if we fall out for a few days.

Another thing to know about me is that I can't keep secrets. I mean to, but I just blurt things out.

Nessa had a sleepover for her birthday. I was so excited and I'd packed my bag all ready to go, but then my legs wouldn't let me climb in the car for Dad to take me to Nessa's house. I was afraid to go and sleep in a house without a night light in the bedroom.

One last thing about school. Miss Struthers says that I am very caring. That's because I can't bear it when

21

anyone falls over in the playground. I always go over and help. My mum says that I should be a nurse when I grow up. I want to be a nurse that works with animals.

Worry

I worry about lots of stuff. Here's my worry list:

- lumpy food
- falling off the balance bench in PE
- not having a partner in class
- getting 0/20 for mental maths
- being asked to talk in class
- being late.

Sometimes I panic and then I can't breathe, so I have to go somewhere quiet and breathe in and out for a bit. Miss Struthers has taught me to do the 555 breathing strategy

– in for the count of five – hold for the count of five – out for the count of five. I can also do the 7/11 strategy. Count to seven breathing in and count to eleven breathing out. That calms me down.

Helpful list

Here are some other strategies that Miss Struthers has given me for my dyspraxia:

- Picturing a task in my head can make it easier.

- Taking a step back when I argue with friends, and trying to see the friends' points of view.

- Walking away if I feel bullied, but let an adult know.

- My mum (who is a drama teacher) has taught me to watch everybody else when I am nervous, to calm me down.

My occupational therapist has asked me to:

- Play with a Rubik's cube or Powerball to improve my fine motor skills.

- Play catch with my mum twice a day while balancing on one leg to help my balance.

Superpowers

Miss Struthers talks to me about feeling good about myself because I don't always focus on the superpowers that come with dyspraxia. These are my superpowers:

- dancing
- karate
- climbing trees
- making collages
- never being late.

Future plans

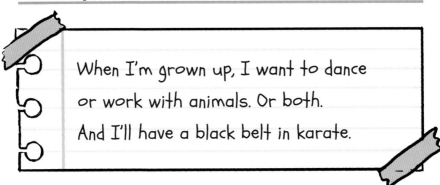

When I'm grown up, I want to dance
or work with animals. Or both.
And I'll have a black belt in karate.

Raj

Hi, my name is Raj and I'm in year four. I live in north London, postcode N17, the home of Tottenham Hotspur, my football team. I have dark hair and green eyes.

I'm in the middle at home. I've got one older brother called Jay, who is in year seven, and a little brother called Arun, who is in year one. I am the smallest boy in my year at school. I'm a very quick runner.

When I was in year R, the teacher noticed that I could not hold a pencil properly to write. Letters and words were all jumbled for me too. So, when I was seven, I went to see a lady who did some tests and found that I have dyslexia and dyspraxia, in equal sizes.

Eva has told you quite a lot about dyspraxia. Dyslexia is not an illness either. I don't always like having dyspraxia and dyslexia. Sometimes they make me feel sad. At times, dyspraxia and dyslexia can be tricky and tiring. At other times, I have two **superpowers!**

Without dyspraxia and dyslexia, I wouldn't be Raj.

My dyspraxia

I've always got bruises because I can't judge space, so I walk into things. That's my dyspraxia. Dyspraxia makes me clumsy too. I break stuff. My mum calls me 'butterfingers' because things always seem to slip between them and break. I don't help my brothers dry the dishes anymore because I broke too many glasses. 😊

I can't catch and I'm not good at throwing a ball where I want it to land. When I was in year two, I couldn't kick a football far. But I wanted to play football like Harry Kane, so I kicked a ball around at playtimes and after school, and my kicking got better and better. I think I must be so good at using my feet to kick a ball because I can't catch it! Now I'm on the A-Team for football. I'm a striker. My mum says **practice makes perfect**.

When I grow up, I want to be a striker for Spurs! Kicking is one of my superpowers.

School

I never stop talking, inside or outside school. That's what my teacher (Mrs Malcolm) says, and that's what my mum says too. I talk non-stop from the minute I wake up until I go to sleep at night.

I love going to school to see my friends, but not for the reading and spelling. That's my dyslexia. It means the words are fuzzy when I read. I can't spell and I get taken out of the classroom to play computer games that help with my spelling. I get 'b' and 'd' mixed up, and so my TA, Miss Jones, gets me to draw a bed with a 'b' at the top and a 'd' at the bottom to help me remember.

I've got a yellow reading ruler to make the text less fuzzy when I read. I like audiobooks, but my mum says I should try to read a bit with my ruler too, for practice. She's going to take me to an eye doctor to get some exercises for my eyes to help with reading.

My handwriting is very small because I don't want Mrs Malcolm to see that I can't spell. My hand cramps when I write because I can't hold the pen properly. That can happen with dyspraxia. I think in pictures, so it's difficult for me to write words. (Mrs Malcolm says that thinking in pictures is a dyslexia thing.)

I am allowed to speak into a school iPad to help me write because I'm never short of words when I'm talking and I know a lot of long words which I can't spell. So the iPad does the spelling for me. Mrs Malcolm says that when I'm older, I will use a laptop all the time to write.

Here are two of my favourite big words:

ACCOMMODATION

PRIVILEGED

Mum says I must be a genius because I'm eight years old and I know bigger words than my brother who is

12. But mum says that's a dyspraxia thing. We are good at storing lots of cool words in our brains.

I like maths a lot. I see the numbers in my head and they have different colours, but I can't tell the time. And I don't know the order of the days in a week. I get muddled.

I can't concentrate in the classroom, so I have to sit at the front where Mrs Malcolm can keep an eye on me. I sit on my hands to stop myself from talking when I should be quiet and listening.

Time

I'm always late for everything. I'm even late when meeting friends or being in the classroom on time after break.

I also miss the school bus some days. My mum goes all pink in the face trying to get me out of my TV chair to pack my bag, but I can't budge.

I never tidy my room, so I can never find the things I need for school. Like my shoes. Or my coat. They are never in the same place twice. I'm the untidiest boy in the school. The head teacher, Miss Green, said that in assembly once when I was being given a football trophy for most goals scored. The whole school giggled and I felt sad. It's because I don't tuck

my shirt in or pull my socks up. What's the big deal? That's what I want to know.

My hobbies

When I'm not playing football, I love making clay models. Then I make clay model animations on my phone. I can be quiet when I'm doing that. It takes hours, and Mum says it keeps me out of trouble.

After all the football and making films, and the non-stop talking at school, I sleep like a log at night.

Gremlins

Sometimes my reading and writing make me feel sad and I don't want to go to school. School can make me very tired, and then I can't focus or remember what the teacher says, and I get a headache from the reading. I don't like being asked questions in class because I can't think quickly like that.

Some days school is great, and I can read; other days my brain feels foggy.

After the holidays I dread going back to school. But then I remember that when I'm at school, I get to hang out with my friends.

Helpful list

This is a strategy that I use for my dyspraxia:

- Practise a lot to get good at things.

And for dyslexia:

- I chunk letters in words using different colours to break words down for reading and spelling.

For confidence:

- I focus on what I know I'm good at. (No one, not one single person in the world, is good at everything.)
- And I remember that there are good days and bad days for dyslexia and dyspraxia.

For worry:

- I count down from 100 in sevens when I feel stressed out.

Superpowers

These are my superpowers:

- I see numbers and sequences of numbers in my head
- football
- model making
- painting
- making films
- using big words
- talking a lot. 😊

Future plans

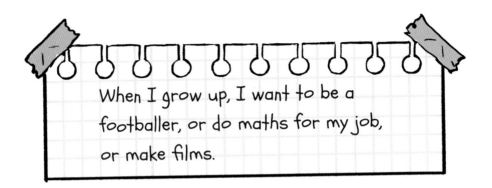

When I grow up, I want to be a footballer, or do maths for my job, or make films.

Leo

Hi, my name is Leonard but everyone calls me Leo. I'm Leo the Lion. I have fair hair and brown eyes. I'm a Scouser because I live in Liverpool which is in the north of England. I live with my dad who is called Roger, my Nana Nell and my older sister, and our stripey ginger cat, Maisie. My sister is called Cassie. She is 13. Sometimes we fight but mostly she is an OK sister.

I found out that I had dyspraxia when I was at the start of year three. I was sent to see a lady called an OT because I fall over a lot and bump into things too. I have bruises all the time, all different colours. Blue, yellow, purple. Any colour you care to mention really. 😊

The OT said that dyspraxia and ADHD can go hand in hand. She said she thought she could see signs of ADHD in me. This was because I didn't always focus on what she was saying. I am very restless too. I fidget a lot and I am a daydreamer. My mum says that I am a **pro** at daydreaming.

I had my ADHD assessment last summer, at the end of year three. I've got the type of ADHD that makes me quiet or bouncy, sometimes both at once. It varies.

Now I am in year four and I'm going to see a foot doctor about my flat feet. The OT said that's a thing that happens with dyspraxia because our muscles can be floppy and we have very bendy joints too. Sometimes my bendy joints feel achy, and Mum has some ointment that I rub on them. Dad says I should join a circus.

My dyspraxia

I am a faddy eater. That's my dyspraxia. I don't like food much at all, but I particularly don't like lumpy foods. I only ate cheese on toast until recently. Now I see a lady who helps me with eating and trying new foods. I still eat a lot of cheese on toast, but I like cherry yoghurt and chicken now. And I'll eat peas and potato waffles but only with tomato ketchup.

I don't like bright light. The lights are too bright at school and it makes it hard to focus. The teacher sits me where there is not a light above my head.

I can't catch and I can't throw. I can't tie my shoelaces either. My mate Patrick was tying them for me, but Mrs Welsby (the TA) said he couldn't do that forever, so now I wear shoes with Velcro bits. I can't run fast either (because of my flat feet, but not because of my Velcro shoes). Mum says that the foot doctor will give me special insoles for my shoes and then I'll be able to run fast. 😊

I can't cross the road safely because I can't judge it and I'm always in too much of a hurry. I'm always first in the queue for the bus, though. My dad says he has no idea how I do that. It isn't difficult. I just edge forward and no one sees me. Queuing for the bus and judging space is easy; crossing roads is not. All this stuff comes with dyspraxia. Well, not jumping the queue, but everything else.

I'm a super swimmer. I swim really fast. I'm half boy, half fish. I've got medals to prove it. It's the only time that I focus, when I'm swimming. Then I really focus and it isn't even hard because I can move so easily.

My other superpower is playing the cello. That was Mrs Welsby's idea. She said that playing an instrument might help my fine motor skills. I picked the cello because it has a lovely, deep sound. School lent me a cello. I dropped it once while I was playing it. I cried, but Mrs Welsby said, 'Not to worry, Leo, it will mend.' I played my cello at the school concert last summer, and I wasn't shy at all in front of all those people. Next summer I'm doing my grade 1 cello exam and I am going to ace it. 😊

Every morning when I get to school, the TA, Mrs Welsby, gets me to do yoga to help my muscles and bones, and my balance. I can't stand on one leg. I fall over!

I know yoga helps my dyspraxia but swimming is my **favourite**. Swimming is my **superpower**.

Friends

My friends are Jack, Charlie, Matt and Lisa (the girl). We ride our bikes a lot, and once, when Charlie dared me to ride with no hands, I fell off and broke my arm. Nan said that my ADHD makes me rush into things without thinking and that I should stop and think before I do anything so silly again.

When we play with other people, I'm quiet. I don't feel like I fit in. But when I'm with my friend group, then I'm noisy. When I'm with a big group, I watch and I try to do what they do. It's called mirroring. That's what the TA said. It isn't easy to copy other people when you are dyspraxic.

My nan said you never know who else is thinking they don't fit in at school, because no one says.

I don't like it when I go quiet, but that's the way I am. Quiet or noisy, with nothing in between – that's me. My school report at the end of year three said **'could speak more in class'**. My dad said, 'That's weird because you never stop talking at home.' But when I do talk in class, the teacher, Mrs Effie, says, **'Stop interrupting, Leonard.'** I can't win.

At parents' evening, Mrs Effie told my dad that I don't look at her in class, so I can't be listening. But I can't listen when I look at people. I listen when I'm not looking. I don't like looking at eyes. I look away.

I'm quiet, but I don't like sitting still. I'm allowed to stand up and stretch in class and I have a toy for when I fidget, and I'm allowed to draw when I listen to the teacher. Mrs Welsby calls it doodling.

School

I quite like school, but I find it hard to focus in class and sometimes, in the afternoon, I nod off at my desk until Mrs Effie shouts, '**Wake up, Leonard**,' and everybody except me laughs. I wish she wouldn't do that.

Handwriting is difficult for me. No one can read my handwriting, not even me. Dad says I scribble, and he's a scribbler too. Mrs Welsby practises writing with me. I can't write the letter 'y' at all, but it's getting better. That's weird because when I was in year one, a lady came into school a bit to help me say the letter 'y'.

I can say most 'y' words now, but I still can't write the letter 'y' and I still have to think before I say 'yellow'.

I didn't read until I was eight years old, then one day I could read all the words. One moment I couldn't read; the next minute I could. I ran around the classroom shouting, '**I can read**!' Then Mrs Welsby took my arm and sat me down at my desk again. I still find it difficult to focus when I'm reading, but I read out loud, very quietly, and that helps. My nan got me an audiobook for my ninth birthday. I liked that a lot. I could listen and focus. Every book should be a listening book.

No one knows where I am in the classroom. Not where I am, but which table to put me at for maths. One week I will get 4/20 and the next I will get 20/20 for mental maths. I move from the bottom to the top table like a yoyo. When I get 20/20, I think I've cracked maths, but it never lasts. One week my dad's proud about my maths; the next week he's mad at me. Mrs Effie says she thinks it's my ADHD. She says, 'Leonard, you are like a flickering lightbulb.'

If I get to practise and really understand my maths, I can remember it in tests and then I'm better at it. I'd drop maths tomorrow if I could. My nan says, 'Just take your time, Leonard, and you will make us all proud.'

I can't always make a start on doing the reading and writing that I'm meant to do in school. And I can't move out of my TV chair at home when I need to do something else like my homework. My dad says that I'm an Arch Procrastinator which makes me sound like a **superhero** but actually means that I keep putting things off.

Mrs Welsby has a tactic for this because she says it will stop everyone from being cross with me if I can stop being a **procrastinator**. I have to pretend to be on a spy mission, then I can get things done.

Organization

Mrs Welsby and Nan work together. Nan has to catch me when I get in the door after school before I can sit down in my TV chair. Then she gets me to tidy my room, pack my bag and line up my clothes and shoes for the next day. If I don't do that, we all have to run around the house looking

for my stuff when I'm meant to be at the bus stop. Everyone gets very cross and Nan says it's a bad start to the day.

After I'm ready for the next day, Nan sits me at the kitchen table with a glass of milk and a chocolate biscuit, and she makes the dinner while I do any homework there is to do. (A world where children didn't have to do homework **ever** would be a better world.)

If I haven't got any homework, then I help Nan to get dinner ready. That's the only other time that I really focus, when I'm helping with dinner. Nan says I'm the neatest cook she has ever worked with. She says, 'You should have seen your mum. The kitchen looked like a bomb had hit it.'

Hobbies

My hobbies are cooking and playing the cello. But my favourite hobby of all is swimming.

Sleep

I can't sleep at
night. Maybe that's
why I fall asleep at
school. Nan gets
me to focus on my
breathing to fall
asleep. Once I'm
asleep, I can sleep
all night. It's getting
to sleep that's tricky, with all   the thoughts going
around in my head, like lots of TV screens are turned
on at once. I'm wired with ADHD at night.

In the morning I can't wake up to an alarm. Everyone
else ends up standing around my bed shouting at me
to wake up, but I'm so sleepy and I don't really like
shouting. So Nan got me a pillow that shakes when
it's time to get up. That wakes me up! I'm up and out
of bed just to escape that scary pillow.

Moods

Dyspraxia and ADHD can affect how I feel too. I get
angry very quickly. Nan says I go from 0 to 20 on an
anger scale in 20 seconds. That's true. Just like your

dad, Nan says. Dad told me to count slowly to 20 and back down and focus on my breathing, in and out. He says he's had to do that forever. Dad is right – breathing and counting help me to stop and calm down a bit so I don't do something rash.

I stopped being invited to birthday parties for a bit because I was so excited. I would bounce off the walls like Tigger from Winnie the Pooh. I'm better with that now I'm in year four, so I'm back on the birthday party lists again. Nan reckons that fizzy drinks give me a sugar rush that makes me too bouncy for a bit before I'm quiet again. 'All of a sudden you crash, Leo,' she says, 'And then we all breathe a sigh of relief.'

Sometimes I feel sad, but never for too long. I bounce back. Dad says I'm re-sil-ient. He says that can be a good thing about being bouncy with ADHD.

Worries

I worry a lot, so I've got a worry board in my room at home with pink, green and orange post-it notes that move around the board for different worries. Nan calls it a traffic light system.

I worry about people laughing at me and about being clumsy too. And I worry about Mrs Effie being cross with me.

A little group of us do mindfulness with Mrs Welsby at the start of the afternoon break. That calms me down a bit because I stop thinking.

When I'm angry, I've got some ADHD music to listen to. That calms me down too.

Helpful stuff

Strategies that work for me:

- I remember better if I say it out loud.
- I read and write better if I say it out loud.
- A fidget toy or doodling helps me focus.
- If I focus on my breathing, it helps me sleep and it helps me feel calmer when I get angry.
- Having a routine helps me stay tidy and keep on top of stuff.
- My worry board and ADHD music calm me down.
- If I pretend to be a Super Spy, I get things done.

Superpowers

I have several superpowers which make me glad that I have dyspraxia and ADHD:

- I'm a grasshopper, so I can do several things at once.
- I'm great at baking.

- I can play the cello.

- I'm like a fish when I'm in water.

- When I focus, I really focus.

Future plans

I might be a chef when I grow up. My dad's a chef. I want to play the cello in an orchestra too.

I will be the greatest swimmer ever and will win lots of medals, and make everyone proud.

ELLIS

Hi, my name is Ellis. I live in Wrexham, home to the best football team in the world. I have reddish brown hair and grey eyes. My birthday is in September and I'm in year five. I have an older sister called Natalie and a little brother called Alex. I'm the middle child. My little brother, who is seven, is autistic without dyspraxia, but I'm autistic and dyspraxic in equal parts. It's hard to see where one ends and the other one begins. Dyspraxia and autism share my life and they are my superpowers. That's how I see it.

I was born Ellie but I stopped feeling like an Ellie in year two, so everyone calls me Ellis now. The one thing I really don't like is wearing skirts or dresses. It isn't the texture, it's the flounce. No one can run as fast in a skirt. I'm only happy when I'm wearing trousers or shorts. Mum lets me choose boys' clothes when we go shopping.

I hated having my hair tied back for school because it made my head ache. As soon as I got to school, I would pull the hair tie out and shake my hair loose for the day. Now I have my hair cut shorter. Mum says, 'Just be yourself, Ellis. You shouldn't have to be anything you don't want to be.'

I found out about the autism and dyspraxia when I was five. I'm not the same as my brother. We are opposites. Busy places and noise don't bother me, but Alex gets very stressed if he has to go to crowded places.

The doctor says I must be hyposensitive. That means I love the noise and lights of the funfair which comes to our town every year. My little brother can't go in the spinning teacups because he gets sick, but I can spin happily for hours, while the rest of my family turns greener and greener. And I rock backwards and forwards because it gives me a buzz. My brother spins and I rock. I've even got my own rocking chair. It helps me think.

My dyspraxia

I break everything I touch. I'm very clumsy. That's one of my dyspraxia things. I can't catch or ride a bike yet. The OT said my hands and eyes won't work together for catching, but if I practise, it should get better. My dad shouts, 'Come on, butterfingers,' when he plays catch with me in the garden. I can put things back together, though. I'm good at that. Dad says that's a superpower. He says it's because my dyspraxia and autism let me focus on the things other people can't see.

I can't balance. Sometimes when I'm just walking along, I fall over. I don't trip, I just fall. When I stand on one leg for the OT, I wobble all over the place. I have been given balance exercises to improve my balance, which will help me with other things too. I have to practise walking tall like a giraffe to make my posture better and stop getting back pain. I love running. I'm a good runner and I'm a fast runner. I run all the stress away and then I feel great.

Dyspraxia and autism can affect my senses. My mum says I'm a faddy eater. I like my food a bit burnt and dry, and I won't eat it unless it is chopped into small pieces. My favourite food is peanut butter and jam toast cut into eight squares.

I don't like being touched and I really don't like human hugs. I think that's my autism.

I've got a giant bear called Alfie from IKEA and I hug him a lot.

My sense of smell is stronger than other people's. I think that's my autism too. Perfume can get on my nerves. And I'll smell burning when no one else can smell anything at all.

Friends

I've got one close friend, Keith, who came to school in year two. He's a lot taller than me. I was lonely before that. I want to have more friends, but I need time alone too.

I know I don't smile, but it doesn't mean I'm not smiling inside. Why do we have to smile? Life isn't that funny. It's hard for me to know what others are thinking. Are they friends or not? Are they cross or in a good mood?

You can't see inside people's minds, that's the problem.

At school, people in my class will talk to me, but I can't always think what to say, and then they walk away.

It's easier to talk at home than at school. I love being with Natalie, my big sister. Natalie is 12 and she is more like a friend than a sister. When I'm with Natalie, I chatter all the time. I wish I could be like that at school, but the words won't come and I go quiet. My Aunty Donna says, 'You can't be friends with everyone, Ellis. Friends are special.'

I can't always hear what is being said. Keith's brother asked me where I live and I said, 'Teddy Bear,' because I thought he asked about my favourite toy. That happens a lot. It makes me feel silly. My dyspraxia can make it tricky to process what I hear – that's why listening is hard. I don't always say words right either. I used to think it was Farmer Christmas. Now I know better. And

when our neighbour's cat died, I thought Daisy the cat had gone to Devon, but really she had gone to heaven.

Mum wants me to see Keith more outside school. But when I get home from school, I need time in my room. It's my quiet space. Mum says I need time to charge my social battery, but it's nice to see friends too.

I don't mind having autism and dyspraxia. I like being me. I'd like more friends, but Mum says that will get easier over time. Miss Strafford, our year five TA, does a circle group twice a week, and that lets me chat more and make new friends at playtime.

School

I'm left-handed when I write and when I use a spoon.
I'm right-handed with scissors and cutlery. My mum
and my sister are left-handers for writing too.
It's a family thing.

I have a pen with a grip so I can hold it right.
My writing is very neat. I am a very neat person.
But my writing is so tiny that no one except me can
read it. Mum says I write like a doll's house child.

I use a school iPad to write. When I speak to the
iPad, it writes what I say. So my tiny handwriting
has worked out well.

Mr Keegan, our year five teacher, says that there is
one word that I use too much. I say 'thing' a lot, but

that's because I can't get to the word I want quickly.
Everyone knows what I mean anyway. Mr Keegan is
too fussy about words, that's the problem.

I could read when I was four but I don't always take in
what I'm reading at school. If I'm tired, I have to read
it again and again which is boring. I like reading my
books, but I don't like reading school books.

Maths is my favourite subject. I love numbers
because I know where I am with numbers.
Sums are either right or wrong. It is very clear-cut.

My mind wanders in lessons a lot. But if I'm interested, then I focus and focus and I can't stop focusing. Mr Keegan, our teacher, says that I hyperfocus. He says that can be a very good thing and will take me far when I can focus on what I really want to focus on when I'm older.

My memory isn't great – that can happen with dyspraxia or autism. I forget where I've put things. When Mum asks me what I did at school, I can't remember, apart from the maths. At times I feel like I am looking at the world through a keyhole. I can't get the whole picture of what's really going on.

My routines

I like my routines. I've got my morning routine on a list stuck to my wardrobe. My night-time routine is on my bedroom door. I'm always ready on time and I can be super early for things.

I always do my homework as soon as I get home. Then it's done and I can do the stuff I want to do. I'm tidy around the house, but my room is a mess. It's my mess, but Mum gets me to tidy my room once a week. She helps me tidy on a Sunday, ready for Monday. But Mum never nags about my room. It's my space.

Hobbies

As well as running, I play the drums. I have a lesson once a week after school and I play in the school band. Drumming is really cool.

I've got another hobby and I do that with my grandpa when we go to see him in Angel Bay on a Saturday. We look out for whales and dolphins in the sea for Sea Watch.

Sleep

I don't like night-time because it's spooky in the dark.
I can't get to sleep because my mind races. When I do
fall asleep, even a tiny noise or light will wake me up.
I got a weighted blanket for my last birthday. It is red
and fluffy, and it helps me sleep better. Our cat, Alan,
sleeps on the blanket and I sleep under it. My dad
got me a blackout blind to keep the sunshine out, so
I don't wake up early now. Dad said he did it for him
as much as for me.

Moods

My little brother gets very angry if there is a change in plans. He goes red in the face and yells, and he throws himself against the wall. Afterwards, he sits in a chair and has a nap. Mum says Alex has meltdowns. If something upsets me at school or if anyone is mean, I just shut down. It is easier not to talk and to just be very quiet. Meltdowns and shutdowns are an autism thing.

Worries

Mum says I'm a terrible worrier. She's right. I worry about everything. How I'm going to get to places, what will happen when I'm there, what could go wrong at any moment each day.

Mum says I have to cut out the 'what

ifs' because you never know what will happen until
it happens.

Tackling stress

My strategies for dyspraxia and autism are:

- using a weighted blanket and blackout blind
  for sleep, and having a cup of water by my
  bed for when I wake up thirsty in the night

- running to de-stress

- following routines to keep me calm.

Miss Strafford helps me with worry. This is what
we do:

- Make a mind map of my worries to take
  a step back from them.

- Count down in fives from 50 for calm.

This is what I have for stress at school:

- A cushion to hug in class.

- A quiet room with blue walls, a lamp and
  a sofa to go to when it is all too much.

- A pebble in my pocket to hold when I want calm.

Superpowers

I have got a lot of superpowers:

- I run really fast and I can run forever.
- I can play the drums for hours.
- I don't need to socialize all the time. I like time to read and game and watch TV or play with my toys alone in my room.
- I love taking things apart to see how they work.
- I'm super organized.
- I can spend hours watching out for whales and dolphins in the sea.
- When I focus, nothing else matters.

If I wasn't dyspraxic and autistic, I don't think I would have these superpowers.

Future plans

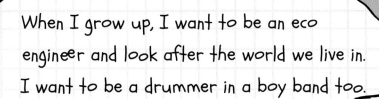

When I grow up, I want to be an eco engineer and look after the world we live in. I want to be a drummer in a boy band too.

Dyspraxia Is Our Superpower
(and Yours Too)

Now you've read about our superpowers, you can think about your superpowers too.

Here are some superpowers that you might have:

- a favourite sport, like running fast or swimming
- making things
- drawing/painting
- playing a musical instrument
- dancing
- singing
- a super hobby
- never being late
- being very neat and tidy
- juggling numbers
- using big words

- hyperfocus
- knowing how things work
- knowing when other people are sad
- enjoying quiet time
- talking to animals
- buzzing with ideas
- having lots of energy
- seeing things other people don't see
- being a bookworm.

Write any superpowers I haven't mentioned here:

- ....

- ....

- ....

- ....

- ....

List of helpful tips

Tips for you:

- Watch other people when you feel anxious.
- A worry board can help with anxiety.
- Practise, practise, practise, and tricky skills will improve over time.
- Remember, there will be good days and bad days. That's life!
- Tell people about dyspraxia.

Some tips for the grown-ups in your life:

- The Dyspraxia Foundation offers very useful advice.

- A physiotherapist can recommend exercises to help with motor skills and balance.

- A podiatrist can help with flat feet.

- An optometrist can help with eye-tracking exercises for reading.

- An online touch-typing course in the school holidays will be fun and a bonus in the long run.

- Routines at home can be helpful.

- A regular place for shoes, coats, favourite toys, schoolbooks, etc. will help avoid the stress of losing things.

What can school do to help?

- Reinforce learning, because once it's secure, a child with dyspraxia can be very able. It might just take longer.

- Remember that children with dyspraxia can be hard to categorize when they are learning.

- There will be good days and bad days, good weeks and bad weeks.

- There will be **eureka** moments!

- Seating is important for focus and writing from the board.

- A sloped board is an aid for handwriting.

- The Dictation app on an iPad can help with writer's block and handwriting.

- Allow fidget toys and doodling for focus.

- Also give opportunities for movement, for focus.

- Routines can be helpful for stress and anxiety.

- A quiet room or quiet space can also help with stress and anxiety.

- A circle group can help with social skills and making friends.

Dyspraxia books for grown-ups

Addy, L. (2004) **How to Understand and Support Children with Dyspraxia**. Cambridge: LDA.

Biggs, V. (2014) **Caged in Chaos: A Dyspraxic Guide to Breaking Free**. Updated ed. London: Jessica Kingsley Publishers.

Boon, M. (2014) **Can I Tell You about Dyspraxia? A Guide for Friends, Family and Professionals**. London: Jessica Kingsley Publishers.

Colley, M. (2006) **Living with Dyspraxia**. Revised ed. London: Jessica Kingsley Publishers.

Hoopmann, K. (2022) **All about Dyspraxia: Understanding Developmental Coordination Disorder**. London: Jessica Kingsley Publishers.

Patrick, A. (2015) **The Dyspraxic Learner: Strategies for Success**. London: Jessica Kingsley Publishers.

Portwood, M. (1999) **Developmental Dyspraxia: Identification and Intervention: A Manual for Parents and Professionals**. London: David Fulton.

Stock Kranowitz, C. (2005) **The Out-Of-Sync Child: Recognizing and Coping with Sensory Processing Disorder**. New York: Penguin.

Van de Weyer, R. and Christmas, J. (2019) **Hands on DCD (Dyspraxia and Allied Disorders): Supporting Children and Young People with Sensory and Motor Learning Challenges**. London: Routledge.

Useful websites for grown-ups

Dyspraxia
The Dyspraxia Foundation:
https://dyspraxiafoundation.org.uk

Dyslexia

The British Dyslexia Association:
www.bdadyslexia.org.uk

Helen Arkell Dyslexia Charity:
https://helenarkell.org.uk

ADHD

ADHD Foundation: the neurodiversity charity:
www.adhdfoundation.org.uk

Additude magazine: www.additudemag.com

Autism

National Autistic Society: www.autism.org.uk

About Us

Alison Patrick

I've been teaching students with dyspraxia, dyslexia, ADHD and autism for many years and, during that time, I've been diagnosed with dyspraxia, ADHD and autism.

I've worked with SEN pupils in a secondary school and I currently work with a social enterprise called Diversity and Ability, tutoring students with SpLDs/ autism, mentoring autistic students and coaching adults in the workplace. I also deliver SEN CPD webinars for PATOSS, and I deliver ADHD workshops for schools.

I'm passionate about improving understanding of SpLDs and autism and making a difference to the lives of neurodiverse people in education and beyond.

Tim Stringer

Tim is an autistic illustrator from North London. Influenced by illustrators Chris Riddell and Edward Gorey, Tim obtained a degree in illustration from the Cambridge School of Art and has worked on everything from book illustration to immersive live games. Outside of illustration, Tim plays acoustic and electric guitar.

Thank You

Thank you to Amy Lankester-Owen for being such a supportive and proactive editor, and thank you to the team at Jessica Kingsley Publishers, especially Laura Savage.

Thank you to Harriet and Roger for reading this through and giving such helpful feedback.

Thanks also to Matt and Will (and not forgetting Nat) for being there for chill-out time when I was writing this book. And a big thank you to Howard (the beautiful black Labrador) just for being a reassuring presence all the time.

Lastly, thank you to Diversity and Ability for being so inspirational and such a wonderful team of people to work with.